Contents

KU-130-431

Any words appearing in the text in bold, **like this**, are explained in the glossary.

This is Israel

Israel only became a country in 1948, but the land has a very old history. This is where the ancient **Jewish** people lived. Christians believe Jesus was born there, and it is also where **Mohammed**, who founded the religion of **Islam**, was said to have risen to heaven. If you took your camera to Israel, you could photograph

places that are special to Jewish people, to Christians and to **Muslims**.

King Solomon's pillars, a group of sandstone rocks are located about 30 km (18 miles) north of the Gulf of Eilat.

A view of Haifa, Israel's most important seaport. It is built on the the side of a steep hill in north-western Israel.

Israel has many interesting cities, including Tel Aviv, Haifa and Jerusalem, a centre of three religions in Israel.

This book will show you some of the old sights of Israel, as well as some of the new cities. It will also tell you much about the country. If you know about the country of Israel before you take your camera there, you will enjoy your visit more.

The place

Israel is a small country located at the eastern end of the Mediterranean Sea, where Europe meets Africa and Asia. This part of the world is known as the Middle East. Israel is about 480 kilometres (300 miles) long and only about 135 kilometres (83 miles) wide.
This is approximately the size of Wales.

Lebanon borders Israel to the north. Syria and Jordan are to the east. To the west is Egypt.

Israel also has some borders that are still to be decided. One of them is the Gaza Strip to the west. Another border that is not final is the West Bank of the Jordan River. The Palestinian people would like to form their own country in the West Bank and Gaza Strip. A third border that still must be settled is the Golan Heights. This land is in the north-east and touches both Syria and Lebanon.

Israel and its Arab neighbours have gone to war many times about these lands. There is still unrest in the region today.

The Negev Desert looks arid, but Israelis have already begun to grow crops in part of it.

Although the country is small, it has a very varied landscape. The Negev Desert in the south covers a little more than half of Israel. It is 12,172 square kilometres (4700 square miles) in size.

In the east is the Dead Sea. This is a large lake at the southern end of the Jordan River Valley. It is called the Dead Sea because it is so salty that nothing can live in it. People like to swim there because it is easy for them to float in the salty water. The Dead Sea is the lowest point on Earth. It is 400 metres below **sea level**.

The Sea of Galilee is the lowest freshwater lake in the world. It is 212 metres below sea level. This lake is also known as Lake Kinneret. It is in the north-eastern part of Israel.

Most of Israel is dry, but sometimes as many as 12.7 centimetres of rain fall in 24 hours. When it rains, dry riverbeds fill up. These are called wadis. When they overflow, the water can cause flash floods and mudslides.

The Dead Sea is about nine times more salty than the ocean.

Jerusalem

Jerusalem, Israel's capital is also one of the country's oldest cities. At least 4000 years old, it has been destroyed and rebuilt several times.

One part of Jerusalem is the walled Old City. If you took your camera to Jerusalem, this is where you would find many sights to photograph, like the Wailing Wall. This wall is all that remains of an ancient **Jewish** temple. Jewish people from all over the world come here to pray.

Christians also come to the Old City. Many visit the Church of the Holy Sepulchre. 'Sepulchre' is another word for tomb. This church was built on the site where the body of Jesus is thought to have been placed before his **resurrection**.

Muslims come to the Old City to go to the Dome of the Rock **mosque**. A mosque is a building where Muslims go to pray. This mosque was built on the place where **Mohammed** is believed to have risen up to heaven.

10

The Wailing Wall (bottom) and the Dome of the Rock mosque (top) are two important places in the Old City.

East Jerusalem is peopled mostly by Israeli-Arabs. West Jerusalem is the new part of the city, where there are many shops and cafés.

11

Places to visit

One of the most popular places to visit in Israel is Masada, a fort near the Dead Sea. In CE 66 a group of **Jewish** people tried to fight against the Romans. At that time, Israel was known as Judea and it was part of the Roman Empire. The Jews fought hard but lost. The Romans controlled the land for many years and renamed it Palestine.

The rock fortress of Masada is more than 2000 years old.

During World War Two, about 6 million Jews died in Europe. Yad Vashem, near Jerusalem, is a memorial to these people. A memorial reminds people of an event or a person that should not be forgotten.

After World War Two, Jewish people wanted a homeland once again in the land that is now called Israel. On 14 May 1948, Israel became a country. This took place in the city of Tel Aviv. Tel Aviv is on the Mediterranean Sea. Many of Israel's neigbours were angry when Arab lands were taken over by Israel. There have been wars in the region ever since.

Boats sail through the harbour at Tel Aviv.

The people

There are almost 6 million people living in Israel. They are known as Israelis, and most Israelis are **Jewish**. In 1950, only a small number of Israel's Jews had been born there. Now that number is larger. Many came from different places, especially after World War Two. Some came from Germany and Poland. More recently, Jewish people have come from Ethiopia and from the former Soviet Union. Israel welcomes all Jews who want to become Israeli citizens.

More than one million of Israel's citizens are not Jewish. Many Israeli-Arabs live there. About 800,000 of them are **Muslim** Arabs. About 170,000 are Christian Arabs. Most Christian Arabs live in the larger cities.

There are also **Bedouins** in Israel. Many of these people are **nomads**. However, some Bedouins now have permanent homes.

Israel has three official languages – Hebrew, Arabic and English. Many people speak Russian and German, too, and some also speak **Yiddish**.

14

Jews pray at the Wailing Wall in Jerusalem.

Life in Israel

Most Israelis live in towns and cities. City dwellers usually live in small flats, though some people who live in the suburbs may have bigger homes. Many homes are now heated by energy from the sun. This is known as solar energy.

Israelis who were born in Israel are called *sabras*. 'Sabra' is a Hebrew word that means 'prickly pear'. This pear is tough on the outside but soft inside. This is the way many Israelis think of themselves.

Some people live on a *kibbutz*. A kibbutz is a farm that is run by people who live there as a community. They share the work and the money they make. They live together and raise their children together.

Many **Muslim** Arabs live in Israel. In Arab culture, hospitality is very important. and it is not unusual for Arab families to invite strangers into their homes for a meal.

Jewish men and women between the ages of eighteen and 21 have to serve in the army. Men must serve for three years while women must serve for two. Older people must serve several weeks each year. Christians and Muslims do not have to serve in the army.

These melons are grown on a kibbutz.

Government and religion

Israel is a **parliamentary democracy**. This means that members of Israel's parliament are elected. The parliament is called the Knesset. It is made up of 120 people who are elected every four years. The president is chosen by the Knesset for five years.

Israel promises religious freedom to everyone. Its ancient sites are sacred to **Jews**, Christians and **Muslims**. The Jewish religion is known as Judaism. Jews who do not practise their faith are known as secular Jews. Most of the Arabs who live in Israel are Muslim, but some are Christian. There are a small number of non-Arab Christians.

Two different kinds of worship: (above) a Muslim in a mosque reads the Muslim holy book, or Qu'ran, and (below) a young man in a synagogue studies the Jewish holy scriptures.

19

Earning a living

Tel Aviv and Haifa are Israel's main centres of **industry**. The major industries are food processing, textiles, chemicals, fertilizers, machinery, electrical goods, armaments and electronic equipment.

Israel has few **natural resources**. The country has little oil, so most must be bought in from Egypt. Israel does have some mineral salts and chemicals.

Outside of the cities, farming is the main occupation. Because there is little rainfall in Israel, farmers use **irrigation** to water their land. Citrus fruits, melons and grapes are important crops.

Farmers in Israel grow fruits, vegetables and flowers.

Guides show monuments to the many visitors who come to Israel.

Many Israelis earn a living from tourism, although the industry has suffered from the many conflicts in the region. Many **Jews**, Christians and **Muslims** come to Israel to visit the holy sites.

21

Schools and sport

In Israel children must go to school from the ages of five to sixteen. Some schools are run by the state. There are also **Jewish** religious schools, known as *yeshivas*, and Arab schools. After the age of sixteen, students can go to the Technion-Israel Institute of Technology in Haifa, or to any one of the six universities in Israel.

Football and basketball are the most popular team sports in Israel. The Maccabeah Games are held every four years. They are known as the Jewish Olympics. Israeli athletes compete with others from around the world.

Swimming is popular because the climate of Israel is so hot and sunny. Israelis also enjoy hiking, cycling and camping. Skiing is popular on the snowy slopes of Mount Hermon on the border between Israel and Lebanon.

Skiing and swimming
are both popular sports
in Israel.

23

Food and festivals

Israelis eat a great variety of foods. These include citrus fruits, lamb, rice and fresh vegetables. All kinds of dishes are popular. This cooking was brought to Israel by people who came there from all over of the world.

Some **Jewish** people observe kosher laws. These laws do not allow them to eat pork, game, shellfish and certain other foods. They also cannot eat meat and dairy products together.

Falafel is a popular Arab food. It is a paste made of chickpeas mashed with oil and then eaten on bread.

Because Israel is important to three different religions, there are three sets of religious festivals in the country. Jewish festivals include **Passover**, **Rosh Hashanah** and **Yom Kippur**. The Jewish day of worship is the Sabbath. This begins at dusk on Friday and lasts until dusk on Saturday. During this period, families spend time together.

A table set for a meal during a Passover celebration.

Christians from all over the world like to celebrate Christmas and Easter in Israel. They often walk along the *Via Dolorosa*, or the Way of Sorrows. Jesus is thought to have walked to the Crucifixion on this path.

During the month that **Muslims** call Ramadan, Muslims do not eat or drink during the daytime. At the end of this month, they have a festival that lasts for three days. It is called **Id-ul-fitr**.

The Future

If you took your camera to Israel, you would see a young country that is still developing. Many trees are being planted throughout the country. This is helping to make the soil of Israel more productive. Through **irrigation**, farmers are able to grow crops in the desert. Israel grows so many fruits and vegetables that it exports, or sells, them to other countries. This brings money into the country. Israel also exports chemicals, among other things.

However, Israel still faces the huge problem of finding peace with its neighbours. For many years there has been a struggle between **Jews** and **Muslims**. The country was founded on land once belonging to Muslim Arabs and for many years Israel has occupied the lands once owned by its Arab neighbours. This has led to years of conflict and bloodshed.

The Israelis and people all over the world are trying to find a solution to this problem, but it will not be easy.

Oranges like these grow in Israel because irrigation has provided water for the plants.

When you arrive in Israel, people may greet you by saying '*Shalom*'. And when you leave Israel, they may say the same thing. This is because the word means both 'Hello' and 'Goodbye'. It also means 'Peace'.

Quick facts about
ISRAEL

Capital ▶
Jerusalem

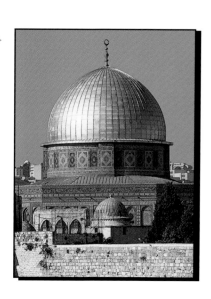

Borders
Lebanon, Syria, Jordan, Egypt

Area
20,770 sq km
(8019 square miles)

Population
6,217,000

Largest cities
Jerusalem (591,400 people);
Tel Aviv-Jaffa (2,181,000 people)

Main crops
citrus and other fruits, vegetables,
cotton, fish, poultry

Natural resources
copper, phosphates, bromide,
potash, clay

Longest river
Loire, at 634 miles (1,020 km)

Flag of Israel

◀ **Coastline**
273 km (170 miles)

Monetary unit
new Israeli shekel

Literacy rate
96 per cent of Israelis can read and write.

Major industries
food processing, diamond cutting and polishing, textiles, clothing

29

Glossary

Bedouin (BEH-doo-in) Arab person that wanders from one area of desert to another, herding camels and sometimes grazing sheep, cattle or goats. 'Badawi' in Arabic means 'desert-dweller'.

democracy type of government in which members of the country's governing body are elected by the people

Id-ul-fitr (ID-ul-fitter) Muslim holiday celebrating the end of Ramadan, the month of fasting. During this festival, Muslims buy new clothes and exchange gifts.

industry making goods and products

irrigation way of watering plants where a farmer directs water to where it is needed

Islam (is-LAHM) religion begun by the prophet Mohammed in the 7th century CE. Muslims believe in one God, Allah.

Jew (JOO) follower of Judaism, a religion that believes in one God and awaits the coming of a saviour, or messiah

Mohammed (moh-HAM-ed) founder of the religion Islam. He was born in CE 570 and died in CE 632.

mosque (MOSK) building where Muslims pray

Muslims (MUHZ-lihmz) people who follow the teachings of the prophet Mohammed and the religion he founded, Islam

natural resources things from nature that are useful to people

nomad (NOE-mad) person who wanders from one place to another, without any permanent home

parliament place where elected representatives of a country meet to make the laws

Passover Jewish festival that celebrates the deliverance of the Israelites from their captivity in Egypt

resurrection (res-ur-RECK-shun) coming alive again after death

Rosh Hashanah (ROSH hash-AH-nah) Jewish New Year

sea level average level of the surface of the ocean. It is the starting point from which to measure the height or depth of any place.

Yiddish (YID-ish) language that is a mixture of German dialects, Hebrew, Central European languages and English. Jews from all over the world speak Yiddish.

Yom Kippur (YOM kip-POOR) Jewish Day of Atonement when Jews fast and seek forgiveness

Index